NATURAL THERAPY

Natural Therapy

Herald Maleske, Ph.D.

THE NATURAL THERAPY FOUNDATION
PRESS
5 Greenleaf, Irvine, CA 92714
(new publisher)

COPYRIGHT © 1976

BY

HERALD MALESKE, M. Div., Ph.D.

Cloth: ISBN 0-87881-042-0
Paper: ISBN 0-87881-043-9
Library of Congress Catalog Number 76-5295

Second Printing
1977

PRINTED IN THE UNITED STATES OF AMERICA

MOJAVE BOOKS
7040 Darby Avenue
Reseda, California 91335

To my wife Dorothy,
who does not need this book,
but whose way of life to a great extent
    inspired it
and confirms the principles that underlie
    the therapy it advocates.

FOREWORD

This is a book that has been written to offer help to those who suffer from emotional and behavior problems. It makes no claim that it will eliminate all such problems, for, as long as we remain human, that is an obvious impossibility. In fact, as you will understand after you read this book, such problems serve a good purpose. When that purpose is recognized and the necessary adjustments made, then the problems are eliminated or at least so modified as to become endurable.

While this book can be helpful to professionals in the field of helping people, it has been written in such a way that its most important information can be understood by almost everyone. This has been done to enable the reader to help himself. The writer is aware that it is often better for those who suffer from emotional and behavior problems, with which they cannot cope, to seek help from others. But it is a fact that the very people who need to do this are often the very ones who usually do not, for reasons that become more apparent after reading this book. There also the sad fact that many counselors are not very successful in helping people because they do not possess the kinds of information about human behavior that are most helpful. To give people an opportunity to help themselves, which so many with emotional and behavior problems are anxious to do, is, therefore, a prime purpose of this book.

Because the writer desires that this book invite a wide reception, he has not only made an attempt to make its contents as easy to understand as possible, but he has also tried to keep it as brief as possible. For those reasons, the highly technical evidence for the assumptions that undergird some of the chief concepts of this book has been omitted. However, for those who wish to examine some of the evidence, a list of helpful books and other materials is supplied at the end of this book.

Also, for the sake of brevity, almost all the illustrative case history that is often included in a book of this kind has been omitted. But there is an even more important reason for this. The writer feels that no two events involving human behavior are alike enough to be helpful in therapy; in fact, it may be harmful to try to compare them. Having read hundreds of books replete with case histories, I have come to the regrettable conclusion that, while an occasional case history may be helpful, many of them are included only to pad a book, details are often exaggerated, seldom is follow-up information given to prove long-term effectiveness of a therapy, and cases involving failure of a therapy are seldom given.

The validity and reliability of the view given here of the origin of emotional and behavior problems and their alleviation rest upon what the writer believes is the best of logical, experimental, clinical, and spiritual sources. The findings of the experimental work of psychologist Hans Eysenck and his associates are the source of the most important scientific concept that underlies this book. The successful clinical experience of psychiatrist Camilla Anderson and psychologist Albert Ellis has tended to confirm the findings of Eysenck. And the spiritual truths that fill the voids in the theories of all of the above are basically those of Biblical Christianity. In the final analysis, however, the views expressed in this book are the result of the distilling of the findings and claims of all of the above and almost every known therapy in the alembic of the life of the author and his thirty years of experience with human behavior as a Lutheran pastor, Air Force chaplain, professor, and social psychologist.

As you read this book, you will note how much I am indebted to the people mentioned above as well as to many others, most of whom are included in the list of references at the end of this book. For their support, encouragement, and contributions to the arduous task of the writing itself of this and earlier versions of this book, I wish to thank also my wife Dorothy, my son Michael, and our loyal friend Patricia Palm. The final version is the result of five major revisions, which included a reduction from about 300 pages to the present highly condensed version.

The reader will note that I distinguish between emotional and behavior problems. Actually, emoting is a form of behavior. But by distinguishing emotion (feeling) from behavior (conduct), I am seeking to treat both the problems that are essentially emotional in their consequences and the problems that are essentially characterized by unacceptable behavior, though elements of both are present in any problem situation. I make this distinction to make this a more useful self-help book. Most self-help books are directed to people who suffer from problems that are essentially emotional (fear, worry, inferiority, etc.) The present book seeks to help also those whose problems are essentially due to the fact that their behavior exceeds the tolerance limits of other individuals, the community, etc., people who are in constant trouble with others, delinquents, criminals, and the like.

Finally, this book is offered as a help for those problems that are primarily functional in origin. For that reason, if you are suffering from emotional or behavior problems with which you have not been able to cope, you should first seek the help of a competent physician to determine whether your problems might be caused primarily from a physical defect. But even if your problems have a primarily organic source, the effects can be ameliorated also through the application of the knowledge contained in this book. While receiving medical treatment, you can also use Natural Therapy as long as any emotional or behavior problems continue to accompany your physical problem.

The writer does not claim infallibility for this book, for human behavior is so complex that no human can fully comprehend it. But if, after a careful reading of this book, you find, as Canon Phillips did about the New Testament after he carefully paraphrased it, that it has the ring of truth, then apply it to your problems. If it helps to eliminate some of them and makes others easier to tolerate, then a lifetime of trying experiences, that were an essential part of the writing of this book, has issued in the glorious — though not entirely unexpected — fulfillment of a divine promise.

H. M.
Irvine, California
Eastertide A.D. 1975

CONTENTS

What's in the Name

Natural Therapy is a fitting title for the approach to emotional and behavior problems advocated in this book. The word "therapy" means healing or, at least, treatment. The word "natural" denotes something which is a part of our nature and is ours by birth; it is also used to refer to something that is both proper and logical.

Natural Therapy finds that emotional and behavior problems have their origin essentially in a characteristic with which an individual is born, something that is part of his hereditary-biological nature. It seeks to alleviate the problems by a treatment that is natural, logical, and proper.

Natural Therapy is, therefore, a name that should invite your investigation and response, for if you are like many people today, you are increasingly aware that there is much in our culture that is artificial, and you long to escape that which is manufactured and contrived and to return to the way things really are and ought to be. In that sense perhaps, Natural Therapy is a therapy whose time has come.

Differences In People Are Natural

Physical differences in people are abundantly evident, and no one denies that such differences are biologically determined. People are born that way. Nature did not leave such an important matter to chance. It is important to the welfare and even survival of humankind that people be able to distinguish one person from another. Think of the confusion that would exist if all people looked alike. It is equally important that people differ in physical strength, in the ways that their organs naturally function, and in many other ways in order to effect the kind of social organization and differentiation that is necessary for progress and even survival. For example, everyone understands what happens when there are all chiefs and no Indians.

2

In short, the very survival of the human race is mute evidence that physical differences are an important part of human nature. If you believe in evolution, then you understand that human survival is evidence that the development of individual physical differences was a biological necessity. If you believe in a Creator, then you understand that divine omniscience would not leave such an important matter as physical differences to chance, but would insure their existence and continuation by placing individual physical differences in the genes and chromosomes of humans.

If all that is true of individual physical differences, why should it not be true of basic personality differences? No one denies that personality differences exist. Neither is it difficult to understand that personality differences are necessary for human progress; yes, even for human survival. For example, for any progress to be made, it is necessary that there be individuals with personalities that lead them to dare to take chances, but it is equally important that there also be individuals with personalities that lead them to check the daring of others, so that they may not go too far and bring harm rather than benefit. The survival of humans often depends on the existence of such differences. Thus again, the existence of basic personality differences is so important that it could not have been left to chance. Evolution or the Creator, as you prefer, insured that they would always exist by making them an important part of human biological nature.

Basic Personality Classifications Have Been Made

Attempts have been made to determine whether certain personality patterns exist, and it is not surprising, in view of the considerations expressed in the previous section, that over the years classifications of basic personalities have emerged. Adding to the contention that differences in basic personality are hereditary-biological is the fact that such classifications, made over the years, have been in remarkable agreement. Since the scientific method consists of observations consistently made by various capable observers, the consistency between basic personality classifications gives them the ring of truth.

4

Hans Eysenck, director of the Institute of Psychiatry at Maudsley Hospital in London, has pointed out the remarkable agreement between classifications made by the ancients and his own findings based upon rigorous experiment. In the following, Eysenck's classification, given in parentheses, fits the classifications of the ancients very well. The early observers of human personality classified people as sanguine (extraverted and stable), choleric (extraverted and unstable), phlegmatic (introverted and stable), and melancholic (introverted and unstable).

Eysenck and his associates have assembled a great deal of evidence that humans have basic personalities according to the amount of extraversion or introversion in their hereditary-biological nature. According to Eysenck's rather well-documented findings, all humans fall somewhere on a continuum ranging from extreme extraversion to extreme introversion. Extraverts are described as outgoing, sociable, impulsive, loud, carefree, aggressive, somewhat unreliable, happy-go-lucky, tough-minded, and optimistic. Introverts are said to be inwardly directed, introspective, quiet, unassertive, reserved, careful, serious, controlled, very reliable, tender-minded, and pessimistic. It is doubtful whether there are any pure or complete extraverts or introverts, for it is likely that everyone possesses, to some degree, qualities of each. Those who possess approximately equal amounts of each are known as ambiverts. The extravert, of course, overbalances in varying degrees on the extravert side, and the introvert, in varying degrees on the introvert side. While no one knows what proportion of the American population is extraverted, introverted, or ambiverted, it would be my guess that the distribution follows a normal, bell-shaped curve, with about two thirds of the population ambiverted and the remaining third about equally divided between the extraverted and the introverted.

Now there is general agreement among people, even among students of human behavior, that a personality trait based on relative extraversion-introversion does exist. There is no general agreement about its origin or its importance. It is the contention of Natural Therapy that this personality trait is hereditary, and it is so important that it determines the basic personality of the individual. Even more important, it is the key to the origin and the solution of emotional and behavior problems.

The Key Factor is Conditionability

Origin and importance are closely related. If something can be demonstrated to be a part of nature, by that very fact it assumes a degree of importance. If we have learned anything in recent years about our world, it is the importance of respecting nature. We have in previous sections, from the viewpoint mainly of human survival, made an initial case for accepting a hereditary-biological source of the existence of basic personality differences in individuals. We now reinforce that contention by tracing the origin of the personality trait known as extraversion or introversion or ambiversion.

I owe the nucleus of the contentions in this paragraph to Albert Ellis, chief exponent of Rational-Emotive Therapy. Suppose we grant for a moment that a personality trait like extraversion-introversion is learned — the result of conditioning by the environment. It would then also have to be granted that the ability to be conditioned is present in humans. The universality alone of condition-ability argues for its hereditary-biological nature. I know of no therapist who denies that conditionability is part of the natural makeup of humans. If it were not true, all of us interested in helping people to change would have to close up shop and forget it. This book, too, would then be an exercise in futility.

At the same time, there is good evidence that the degree of conditionability is also inherited. No one denies that there are differences in degree of conditionability among individuals, and, if conditionability is inherited, certainly the differences in condition-ability are quite logically also biologically determined. And this is what we observe everywhere. Often children in the same family display differences in degree of condition-ability. Again, it is Hans Eysenck who has gathered a great deal of evidence from scientific studies to support the view that the degree of conditionability is inherited, evidence, for example, from the studies of identical twins reared in differing environments. (Refer to some of his writings listed in the references for more information on this.) It is

Eysenck's feeling that the degree of condition-ability is controlled by the reticular formation of the central nervous system. Ellis, too, in his wide experience in psychotherapy, has been led to conclude that the degree of conditionability is something with which people are born. (See also his writings.) As one would expect, the best evidence for variable conditionability as a biological inheritance has emerged from studies of delinquent and criminal behavior.

Eysenck's major findings in this area are that extraverts are difficult to condition, while introverts are easily conditioned. In addition, he has also found that both extraverts and introverts are highly emotional. It seems to me that it is more helpful to view these phenomena in the following manner. Difficult-to-condition individuals develop extravert characteristics, and easily-conditioned individuals develop introvert characteristics. Both the difficult-to-condition and the easily-conditioned individuals develop a compulsion to feel and behave as they do, and the force of this compulsion makes them highly emotional individuals. All this becomes more clear later in this chapter.

Because of the compulsion engendered by the degree of conditionability, it is easy to understand how degree of conditionability determines the basic personality of the individual. This factor, too, argues for the hereditary-biological nature of degree of conditionability, for if evolution or the Creator decreed that basic personality had to be a part of nature, then that which produces basic personality must also be under biological control.

The primacy of the hereditary-biological nature of the degree of conditionability present in any individual is the most important determinant of human behavior. Eysenck holds that the hereditary-biological nature of an individual is 80 percent responsible for the nature of his behavior. Ellis boosts that to 85 percent. It is no accident that increasing study of the nature of the human organism is pointing more and more in the direction of the primacy of the biological determinants of human behavior. It should come as no surprise, then, that in Natural Therapy we find the key to the origin and the solution of emotional and behavior problems in the degree of conditionability with which an individual is born.

Degree of Conditionability
Produces Problems

When one is easily-conditioned, under certain environmental conditions one will develop problems that are experienced primarily as emotional, though some behavior problems may also occur. When one is difficult-to-condition, one will become involved with problems produced by one's unacceptable behavior although emotional problems may also occur. When one is neither too-easily-conditioned nor too-difficult-to-condition, one will experience both emotional and behavior problems, though usually of only a mild variety; one's most common problem will be related to boredom. In these three different types of personalities, you will have recognized the introvert, the extravert, and the ambivert, as Eysenck classifies them.

Easily-Conditioned People
Have Emotional Problems

If you have significant emotional problems, it is basically because you were born as a person who is easily conditioned. You are easily influenced, easily impressed, highly suggestible, and you take things very seriously. Ellis would say, in his usual blunt but highly accurate manner, that you are gullible. The result is that you exaggerate the importance of everything that concerns you, even remotely.

It is not those things that happen to you or in any way concern you that produce your emotional problems. It is the exaggerated way in which you look upon them that causes your emotional problems. Let me explain how this unfortunate and inborn habit of exaggeration causes your emotional problems.

Camilla Anderson, prominent psychiatrist, who once served as chief psychiatrist at the California Institution for Women, has developed a theory of grandiosity, parts of which I have modified to fit into my own view of the origin of problems, which I describe here and in the following section. When you were a child, even the ordinary care, love and concern that parents and other significant people manifested to you made you feel special and important. If they were overconcerned, as they likely were, and overprotected you, you felt extra-special. If they spoiled and pampered you, your feelings of self-importance knew no bounds. But what if your parents neglected you and even abused you? If you were not easily-conditioned, you probably would have felt that it was unfortunate, but you would have accepted it. But because you were easily-conditioned, you felt it was horrible, and you felt compelled to defend yourself against it and to overcompensate for it by developing a feeling of superiority (see Adler's writings in the references). So, no matter how you were treated, you could not help feeling special and important. And you would take very seriously anything that might threaten that self-feeling.

In addition, you developed a value system which you took so seriously that you could not stand any failure to live up to it. The value system, of course, consisted primarily of anything that pleased your parents, who were regarded as super-people by you. In addition, your religion teachers also taught you what pleased God, who controlled everything about your life. No wonder, then, that you felt you just had to be perfect and felt a compulsion to act in a manner that could not be faulted in any way.

You see, you were setting up impossible conditions for yourself, and serious conflicts were bound to arise. Your grandiose ideas about your own importance would sooner or later be threatened by physical harm in the form of injury or illness or just the fear of them. Your grandiosity would be threatened when others failed to show you the honor and deference to which you felt entitled or when you feared that would happen. Similarly, you felt threatened when you did not act perfectly or even when you feared that you might act imperfectly in a particular situation.

The result of all this was that fear and resultant inferiority were constantly present in your life. You feared other people. You feared that you would fail in your performance. So you generally stayed away from people who posed a threat to you, tending to generalize and withdraw from people in general. You also feared that you would not perform perfectly, so, to avoid failure, you preferred not to perform at all, remaining silent, quiet, inactive, unassertive, taking no chances at all.

As long as you remained in the protection of a secure home, you could get by with this withdrawal from people and performance. But when the security of the home was threatened by marital strife, divorce, alcoholism, and the like, the threat to your grandiosity increased to the point where you developed significant emotional problems primarily, producing behavior problems secondarily. I do not feel expert enough to discuss problems at that level, and anyway, you are now more interested in your adult problems, so we continue.

But when you must do without much of the security which a stable home life has brought, the threat to your grandiosity increases more than ever before. For most of you, that began at the time of adolescence. The experience of the new drive associated with sex, the desire for independence and the fear of it, the need to learn self-control, and especially the beginning of what has been called formal operational thought, which enables one to conceptualize the thoughts of others — all these and other new experiences that enter life at this time combine to force the adolescent to focus his thoughts mainly upon himself more than ever. He is acutely self-conscious. He holds the mistaken notion that others are as concerned about him and interested in his appearance as he is. He imagines that he is the focus of everyone's attention. In all this you can readily understand that your original grandiosity, now nourished by adolescent egocentricity, increased markedly, and your emotional problems associated with fear and inferiority also escalated.

But most of you could fall back upon a secure home, adolescent egocentricity diminishes at age 15 or 16, and you learned to develop enough defense mechanisms to keep your emotional problems fairly well under control.

As the years passed and you were forced by social custom — which for you is more a compulsion than a custom—to become independent of the home, threats to your grandiosity came more frequently and became more difficult to handle. Young adulthood poses new threats as new demands are made — the demand for physical intimacy, for choosing an occupation, for defining one's proper role. You may have become confused, apathetic, unable to work, overcritical, upset, and angry, often at the slightest provocation.

It is at about this time that some of you began to experience the significant emotional problems with which you are still finding it difficult to cope. Others of you first began to experience them later in adult life. At this point it is appropriate to describe just what usually occurred.

Recalling that, with your ease of condition-ability, you exaggerated your own importance as a person and your need to behave properly, as an adult you were now fully responsible for yourself and your behavior. Any threat to your feelings of self-importance and your expectation that you must behave properly now assumed more ominous proportions. In addition, now more fully exposed to the vicissi-tudes of life, the number and variety of threats increased significantly. Sooner or later a conflict situation was bound to arise in which you found yourself unable to be or to perform as you felt that you just had to be or had to perform.

The conflict may have resulted from a dis-appointing love affair, an incompatible marriage, a serious illness, a promotion in your job, a lack of a promotion in your job, an enforced separation from loved ones, a failure to achieve academic goals, and a thousand similar stressful situations. But the conflict always consisted of your inability to be as good, attractive, well-liked, wise, successful, looked up to, catered to, perfectly healthy, secure, etc. as you felt you had to be, or to behave as correctly, perfectly, acceptably, etc. as you felt you had to behave. It was all made worse because, as a grandiose person, you felt that it must not have happened to you, and, because it did, you exaggerated its importance. To you it was not just unfortunate, sad, tough luck, or part of life; you considered it to be awful, terrible, horrible, and catastrophic.

At this point something should be said to explain a phenomenon that may be puzzling to the reader. Since the problem here is exaggeration of importance, why wouldn't an easily-conditioned person exaggerate the good things that happen to him and thus offset the exaggeration of threatening things? No doubt that does happen to a certain extent. But the reason that impressionable people are more concerned about the negative things that happen to them is that the emotion of fear produces more powerful reactions than feelings of security and elation.

Unable to be or to act as you felt that you had to, you felt acutely threatened, and your body, operating as it has been designed to do, started the adrenalin and other hormones flowing, preparing you for fight or flight. You felt angry — yes, even enraged — but you had been led to believe that anger and rage are unacceptable forms of behavior, so you repressed them, and they continued to add more hormones. You felt resentment, and the hormones continued to flow. You felt guilty. This is not normal guilt for wrong-doing; this is neurotic guilt — guilt because you cannot forgive yourself, guilt which is exaggerated; it may even be guilt for wrong-doing which has not even occurred; it is self-reproach and self-blame — and the hormones kept flowing. You felt helpless and you became afraid, and the hormones flowed more abundantly than ever.

The constantly-called-for but unused adrenalin and other hormones kept the organs in your body in constant tension. You developed headaches, muscle spasms, stomach troubles, insomnia, and other minor physical symptoms. And when your conflicts continued or increased, additional and more frightening symptoms began to appear. You suddenly felt weak and faint, your heart began to palpitate, you found it difficult to breathe, you began to fear that something dreadful was happening to you, that you were losing control, and that you would go to pieces. And you went into panic.

Oh, you got over the panic all right, but from then on you could not get rid of the fear of panic. As Claire Weekes has described it (see her books listed in the references), your nerves had become sensitized, going into action at any hint of fear and overreacting more than they ever did. All this led to new fears, fear of insanity, phobias (claustrophobia, agoraphobia, etc.), obsessions, feelings of unreality, almost complete loss of self-confidence, high suggestibility. In general, there arose a fear of the symptoms produced by the original fear. Thus, a vicious circle was set up by which your emotional problems perpetuated themselves. Your overworked endocrine glands became fairly exhausted, and you began to feel depressed. Perhaps at this point, or even much earlier, you began to drink or take drugs.

The description above of the origin and development of your emotional problem is a general one. The various steps and symptoms do not always occur, nor do they always occur in that order. But I am certain that somewhere you found your own problem described. An understanding of the origin of your problem is an important step in learning to cope with it. Help for your problem is suggested in the next chapter, and I would advise you to turn immediately to chapter two, while I go on with the task of helping those with essentially behavior problems to understand the origin of their problems.

Difficult-to-Condition People Have Behavior Problems

If you have significant behavior problems, it is basically because you were born as a person who is difficult to condition. You are not easily influenced by people or things that happen to you. You don't take things — people and events — seriously enough. The result is that you underestimate the importance of everything in which you are involved.

It is not those things that happen to you or involve you in any way that produce your behavior problems. It is your inability to take them seriously enough that causes your behavior problems. Let me explain how this unfortunate habit of underestimating and minimizing the importance of things that involve you produces your problems.

Like the person with the essentially emotional problems, as a child you developed feelings of grandiosity about yourself, but in an altogether different way. The love and care bestowed upon you by your parents made little impression upon you. Even any neglect or abuse failed to phase you very much. In other words, your self-feelings did not to any great extent depend upon influences from without.

Since you could not be conditioned from without to any appreciable degree, the factors that exercised the most control over you came from within, from your perceived and felt drives and needs. Now, easily-conditioned people also are influenced by their needs and drives, but because of the conditioning of their parents and teachers in the interest (as they conceived them) of the demands of God and society, their drives and needs were subordinated to the approval of God and society, and it was from that they gained their feelings of grandiosity.

As a difficult-to-condition individual, however, your own drives and needs had priority over the approval of God and society, and you derived your feelings of grandiosity from them. By the fact that they were virtually unopposed, your drives and needs and their satisfaction became paramount. Thus you were led to elevate yourself and your importance in your own eyes. Nothing was more important to you than the satisfaction of your own drives and needs. And this is plainly a form of superiority and grandiosity.

Because your drives and needs had priority, they exercised such a powerful influence that their satisfaction became the center around which your value system revolved. What satisfied your drives and needs became your value system. And, because drives and needs are indeed powerful, your need to behave in accordance with their demands became compulsive. You just had to satisfy them by hook or crook.

And, of course, it was inevitable that your behavior would get you into trouble, both with those like you who felt just as compelled to have their drives and needs fulfilled above all else, and with those unlike you who felt that the satisfaction of drives and needs should be subordinated to the demands of God and society. Already, as a child you were basically unruly and disobedient. If your parents had the proper insight and courage, they tried to exercise strict discipline, and this may have modified your unacceptable behavior to a degree, but you remained basically a difficult child. Most likely, however, in conformity with the prevailing custom of the age, your parents were permissive and did not take the necessary disciplinary measures, and your unacceptable behavior continued and your grandiosity remained intact. In fact, your parents may have even spoiled and pampered you, despite your repaying them with difficult behavior, and your grandiosity soared and your irresponsible behavior with it.

You were a problem to your teachers and to others in authority. You might also have even become, at an early age, a juvenile delinquent. When you reached adolescence, when your ego-centered drives and needs increased, your behavior became a real problem to many more people. You rebelled completely against your parents, and you may have run away from home, used drugs for kicks, indulged in disapproved sexual behavior, joined gangs of toughs, indulged in criminal behavior such as robbery, theft, assault, etc.

As you grew into adulthood, you may have advanced to more serious crime and landed in jail. If you did not get involved with the law, you at least caused a great deal of trouble for yourself, but especially for others, by your behavior. You may have become an alcoholic because of the kicks that excessive drinking brought you. You may have caused trouble at work with your bosses and fellow workers because you insisted on having your own way. You might have even reached the top in the business or political world, but you were ruthless and unconcerned about other people and even about the law. In your marriage you probably used your spouse almost exclusively for the satisfaction of your own needs, and most likely you were not interested in your children unless they could satisfy your own drives and needs above all else. You may have received a large number of traffic tickets, most of which you probably ignored. You no doubt used your friends, if you had any, only to satisfy your own exclusively selfish goals.

As a result of all this and many other forms of undesirable behavior, you were constantly defeating yourself. You became the slave of your desires and needs, and the harder you tried to get them satisfied, the more frustration you experienced. As might be expected, others would not generally cooperate for any length of time to give you the kinds of responses to which you felt entitled. They would not continue to give without receiving anything in return. In fact, some refused to tolerate your selfish behavior. So they turned away from your exploitations, ignored you, or even opposed your self-centered efforts. As a result, your adrenalin and other hormones began to flow.

Your first reaction was hostility. You hated people for their lack of cooperation and acceptance. And when this did not help, your hostility turned into rage. You would not put up with this unfair treatment. Your failures were all the fault of others. It was all unjust, and you seethed within. You struck out blindly at your enemies. You lost a great deal of whatever control you had of your behavior, until your behavior exceeded the tolerance limits of the community. You were in deep trouble.

During all this, your accumulated tensions brought about a great many physical symptoms, many of them similar to the ones that the easily-conditioned individual experienced during stress. Some of you dealt with your conflict by trying to resolve it by withdrawal into some kind of conversion hysteria — you developed an imaginary physical disability.

Keep This in Mind

In the description of the origin and development of emotional and behavior problems given above, no doubt you became aware that you had experienced both kinds of problems. That is because seldom is an individual so easily conditioned that on occasion some drive or need may not come through so strongly that a behavior problem will result; one's grandiosity will also contribute to that. And seldom is an individual so difficult to condition that he will not on occasion experience some compulsion to behave in a manner demanded by God or society and which will produce an emotional problem for him; his grandiosity will also contribute to that. A moderately-conditionable person (a so-called ambivert) experiences both kinds of problems, but they assume only moderate proportions, and, because a high degree of compulsion (emotion) is not present, they are generally easy to cope with. The failure to recognize these phenomena has led many therapists to overlook basic differences in degree of conditionability that are at the basis of problems. When these exceptional problems do occur in the life of easy-to-condition and difficult-to-condition individuals, they also are usually of a minor nature, and it is still the basic degree of conditionability in the individual that needs to be dealt with.

Keep in mind also that the greater the degree of conditionability, the more difficult the emotional problem is likely to be. Similarly, the lesser the degree of conditionability, the more difficult the behavior problem is likely to be. How to deal with the degree of conditionability and the emotional and behavior problems it produces is the subject of the remainder of this book.

Chapter Two

*NATURAL THERAPY
AND THE
ALLEVIATION OF
EMOTIONAL
AND
BEHAVIOR PROBLEMS*

These Are Some Preliminary
Considerations

It is quite understandable that emotional and behavior problems of ambiverts, or individuals with only an average or moderate amount of conditionability, should tend to disappear more or less spontaneously, even without treatment. In other such cases, where a severe conditioning through the environment has produced problems for a person of moderate conditionability, the discovery of the part that such conditioning has played and a therapy based on some appropriate reconditioning are often able to bring about significant relief from such problems.

But where emotional and behavior problems occur basically because of easy or difficult conditionability, and when treatment is directed toward trying to change that inborn

31

conditionability, treatment is likely to be largely unsuccessful. Simply to try to get serious-minded people to take things less seriously is only minimally successful. To try to get people who do not take things seriously enough to take things more seriously is also only minimally successful. And there are good reasons why such conditionability will not yield to modification to any great extent. After all, if evolution, the Creator, or the Creator working through evolution, whichever is your conviction, saw to it that a degree of conditionability should be a part of the biological equipment of humans, and did so to insure both the survival and improvement of the human race, you would certainly expect that such conditionability and the personality traits it produces would not yield to modification to any great extent.

Other therapy, directed at the emotional and behavior problems themselves, is also largely unsuccessful because it is not directed at grandiosity. To try to persuade an individual suffering from inferiority resulting from grandiosity produced by easy conditionability to accentuate his good qualities and to accept his weaknesses is largely an exercise in futility for a grandiose person. To try to help a person to overcome his behavior problems resulting from grandiosity produced by difficult conditionability by minimizing them, forcing the person to act responsibly or trying to change the environment may work temporarily but not permanently.

There is only one way to insure mastery over emotional and behavior problems, and that is the natural way. The natural way is to use basic conditionability for the purpose that nature intended. Up to this time, those with emotional and behavior problems have been using their basic conditionability primarily for the wrong purposes. Of course, it is to be used partly for the individual's own survival and general well-being, but it has been given primarily for the survival and welfare of others. Problems arise when individuals use their basic conditionability primarily for their own aggrandizement, for promoting primarily their own interests, for nourishing their own grandiosity.

While basic conditionability, since it is part of nature, cannot be greatly modified, grandiosity, which is due to conditioning, can. When one's behavior harmonizes with nature, then grandiosity disappears, and everything about the individual functions as it was intended. When the easily-conditioned individual fulfills the purpose of his conditionability and uses it primarily to benefit others, then grandiosity diminishes because he is able to accept himself, for he is now functioning the way he is supposed to. His grandiose need for being perfect — a reaction to his guilt for not doing what he should be doing — largely disappears as he now does what he should be doing. His grandiose need for entitlement diminishes as he experiences real self-esteem which comes from contributing to life what one can. And, in the process, he receives what he vainly sought before: the esteem of others.

When the difficult-to-condition individual fulfills the purpose of his conditionability and uses it primarily to benefit others, then his grandiosity also diminishes, for his greatest drive and need is fulfilled: the need for the cooperation of others to have all his legitimate needs met. No longer does he grandiosely have to ignore the needs of others and indulge in unacceptable behavior to get his needs met. Grandiosity is largely replaced as he realizes that he is able to have his needs met best as he uses his abilities to meet the needs of others. And in the process, he receives what he vainly sought before: greater freedom of behavior.

Of course, to use conditionability primarily for the purpose for which we have it is not easy to do, and as long as we are human we can do so only imperfectly. While it is generally true that we will experience relief from our problems in the degree that we are able to use our conditionability correctly, practically everyone should be able to learn to use his conditionability correctly enough to cope with his problems. The important thing is to know what to do and then set about doing it as best we can.

Both easily-conditioned and difficult-to-condition individuals can find an almost endless variety of ways in which mankind can be helped, but there are, in addition, special areas in which one or the other can function more effectively. In general, easily-conditionable individuals are especialy equipped to recognize, point out, show compassion, motivate, persist, pay attention to detail, be more careful when there is a need to improve the lot of mankind. Difficult-to-condition individuals can help especially to supply the necessary courage, optimism, aggressiveness, daring, and the like, which are often necessary to go into real action in any endeavor to better our world.

For some of you, especially those of you whose problems are only recent ones, what has been stated thus far about therapy should be enough for you to go right into action and get almost immediate results in modifying your problems. But for most of you, especially those of you who have been battling your problems for some time, it is best to go about dealing with your problems in a more deliberate and systematic way. After all, you got into your problem through your wrong thinking, which became habitual and deeply ingrained through constant repetition over the years. To control your problem, you basically have to change your habitual way of thinking before you can effectively change your actions. The suggestions given in the remainder of this chapter will help you.

Acquire an Adequate Religious Outlook!

Every survey that has been made in our country on the subject has indicated that an overwhelming majority of the population claims to believe in the existence of God. What is more natural, then, than to start dealing with our problems on the basis of this almost universal belief? In addition, experience has demonstrated that the most effective therapy for emotional and behavior problems is an adequate religious outlook. Almost every pastor has seen or known of incidents in which a person with such a problem has overcome it through an adequate religious outlook, sometimes even instantaneously. By an adequate religious outlook, I mean a religious faith that is properly applied to the special needs of individuals with a high degree or a low degree of conditionability.

Very likely you are one who has tried religion, and it has apparently failed to help you in your problem. Perhaps you feel that you have not been able to acquire a religious faith, let alone an adequate religious outlook. Or you feel that you have a religious faith and even a religious outlook that seem otherwise to be adequate, but somehow they have failed to help you sufficiently with your problems.

For those of you who wish to have a religious faith and an adequate religious outlook, and for those of you who wish to have the religious faith and outlook you presently have to help you more with your problems, I have included a special chapter that follows this one in which I treat the subject rather thoroughly.

I append such a chapter for several reasons. I believe with Carl Jung that an adequate religious outlook is the final answer to problems like these. Second, the various factors that enter into acquiring such an outlook are often unknown and require rather thorough explanation. And third, I feel that the spiritual area is the area of my greatest experience and the one in which I can help you most effectively.

So, if I have convinced you to give spiritual remedies a first or an additional try, turn immediately to chapter three. If you have given up on the spiritual, however, there are still other ways to gain a great deal of control over your problems, and they are described in the remainder of this chapter.

Switch the Focus to the Real Problem!

Here again it is to be noted that it is certainly unnatural to think that you can solve your basic problem by being preoccupied with other problems. So the next direction is to return to the nature of your real problem, as we now go on to suggest.

Before you can successfully tackle your real problem, you first have to remove all the additional factors that have grown up about it to complicate it and almost obscure it. For one thing, after reading the previous chapter, you, who are having mainly emotional problems, must quit blaming yourself. And you, whose problems are mostly behavioral, must quit blaming others. Because the problems of both of you are basically the result of widespread ignorance of how to properly use the kind of conditionability with which you were born, no one is really to blame. In fact, you can even give your sagging spirits a lift by reminding yourself that you possess qualities that are important to the improvement and survival of the human race and, as soon as you can get a handle on the solution to your problems, that you will be able to better use the kind of conditionability you possess to do your part in such improvement and survival. Thus, the knowledge of the cause of your problem should stop you from adding to it and obscuring it through self-blame and scapegoating.

Perhaps the most important factor complicating your situation is your preoccupation with the secondary problems produced by your real problem. So fearful, painful, and disturbing are the emotional and behavior problems themselves and their bizarre and frightening physical effects, that they steal the spotlight and become the object of most concern, and your real problem (the failure to properly use your conditionability and the grandiosity that results from such failure) goes untreated.

Here is what often happens. The easily-conditioned individual, who feels compelled to act in an impossible way, develops severe emotional symptoms. These emotional problems, together with their physical effects, become so fearful and painful that they become the object of principal concern, and this creates additional emotional and physical problems, forming a vicious circle and leaving out any possibility of dealing with the real problem: the failure to properly use his easy conditionability and the grandiosity caused by this failure. Similarly, the difficult-to-condition individual, who feels compelled to satisfy his own drives and needs above all else, develops unacceptable forms of behavior. This undesirable behavior is condemned and punished, and the individual reacts to these consequences with resentment, hardening of attitude, hostility and rage, which, in turn, produce additional undesirable behavior and also physical symptoms, creating a vicious circle and leaving out any possibility of dealing with the real problem: the failure to properly use his difficult conditionability and the grandiosity produced by this failure.

Now these vicious circles must be broken to prevent the emotional and behavior problems and their physical effects from usurping your attention and concern. Claire Weekes, the Australian physician who has written several books related to this problem (these books are listed in the references), urges people with emotional and consequent physical problems to do four things about them: face them, accept them, float past them, and let time pass. The heart of her advice seems to be the acceptance of the secondary problems and symptoms. But, in my experience, I have found that sufferers find that difficult to do, unless they have some good reason to do so. Weekes supplies one reason: she assures the emotional sufferer that the problem won't get any worse. But the secondary problems and their physical effects are often so unnerving that it's hard to believe that they won't get any worse. A big drawback to whatever advice Weekes gives is that she holds that the original problem or cause of the secondary problems and symptoms is largely unknown and unknowable.

My advice regarding secondary problems and symptoms is to try to accept them, but to do so because there is a known cause (the failure to properly use one's degree of conditionability), and this can be so modified that the resulting problems will either disappear or at least be controllable, no matter how long they have persisted. So stop fighting your emotional and behavior problems and their physical symptoms in the way that you have. That only keeps them in the center of the stage, perpetuating them, and even escalating them. Accept them for what they are: the result of emotional and behavioral reactions to your failure to properly use your inherited conditionability. If you persist in such realistic and understanding acceptance, you will gradually lose your preoccupation with them, and you will find them less and less able to control you, and you will be able to give more time, attention, and effort to dealing with your real problem, which, at this stage, you should be convinced is your failure to properly use your relative conditionability and the grandiosity that results from that failure.

It is interesting to note here that Weekes, who has treated thousands of people suffering from nerves, states unequivocally that a religious faith will cure such conditions, but she intimates that only the fortunate ones are able to acquire such a faith and that even those with faith often have to be shown how to use it under such conditions. At any rate, in the absence of such a faith or the knowledge of how to use it, do try to take enough of the tensions out of your emotional and behavior problems and the resulting physical symptoms by accepting them, mainly by accepting them as they are now. That also means not adding to their perpetuation or growth by blaming yourself or others, and diminishing them by accepting them for the time being.

If you are still so upset that you cannot focus your mind clearly and for any length of time on anything but your immediate situation, then you might try physical relaxation. There is no doubt that, while it is generally acknowledged that the mind largely controls the body, it is not so generally known that the body can also control the mind. Edmund Jacobson, an M.D. and a psychiatrist, over many years has assembled a great deal of evidence to show how relaxation of the body is able to produce relaxation of the mind, resulting in both healthier bodies and healthier minds. I have been particularly impressed with Jacobson's contention that control of mental activity becomes possible by relaxing tension in those parts of the body that produce speech, particularly the tongue and the eyes.

In my attempt to keep this book brief, I will not include any descriptions of techniques of relaxation that might help you rid yourself of undesirable tensions, but I do refer you to Jacobson's books which are readily available (two of them are listed in the references). While relaxation of the body is not difficult to accomplish, it is my experience that keeping the body under sufficient relaxation to produce prolonged release from undesirable tension requires the kind of practice and discipline that the average individual finds too demanding. However, I do recommend that you give physical relaxation a consistent try.

It has also been advocated by many that relaxation from tension may be obtained through physical exercise, and there is little doubt that this is true. Others have suggested that keeping occupied at tasks or activities that distract the mind from tension-producing thoughts will also tend to relieve tension. In the measure that they tend to focus your attention away from immediate problems that are not your real problem, they can be helpful to you and should be used while you initiate a program designed to deal adequately with the problem that is basically causing them.

If, even after following the previous suggestions, you are still so upset and unnerved that you cannot seem to rid yourself of your preoccupation with your emotional and behavior problems and their physical effects, then ask your physician to prescribe sedation for you, just for the time being, sufficient to enable you to keep your real problem in sufficient awareness, so that you will be able to put into practice the remedies given below that are designed to help you cope with it. While the use of sedatives may make your immediate problems seem less severe, don't be tempted by this measure of relief to discontinue the faithful use of all the suggestions made in this chapter.

When you are able to get yourself in hand enough, even if only to a small degree, to keep your focus, whenever necessary, on your real problem — your failure to properly use your conditionability and the grandiosity that results from that failure — then you are well on the way to learning to cope with your emotional and behavior problems and their physical effects. But this is only a start. You must from now on, until it no longer produces significant problems, keep your mind focused on the real problem whenever any sign of an emotional or behavior problem or its physical effects appears.

No matter what the fearful feeling, the trouble-producing behavior, even the physical sensation that you may experience, insist to yourself that, until you can determine the true state of affairs, whatever problem it is creating for you at the moment, this is due only to your failure to properly use your conditionability. So, what you must do at the very first intimation that your hormones are going into action and stirring up your emotions unduly is not to try to fight the rising tide of your emotions. That only escalates them. The thing to do is to take the wind out of their sails by saying to yourself: "It's only a reaction from improperly using my conditionability again! Go ahead and get it out of your system!"

You see, what you are doing when you turn the focus immediately upon the real problem is that you are stopping the emotions from continuing to rise. How? By switching the focus from a problem which appears dangerous and threatening to one that can be controlled and is thus really harmless. After, through Natural Therapy, you have learned to correct the real problem, that is all you will have to do to turn off your emotions should they ever, as a result of habit, act up again.

But at the beginning, while, for a moment, the change in focus from a threatening situation to one that is not threatening will temporarily stop the rising tide of emotion, the focus will quickly tend to revert to its former threatening situation, and emotions again will tend to rise. So it will be necessary to take additional measures to maintain focus on the real problem. How this can be done is the subject of the next section.

Before continuing with that, however, it is helpful to clarify what actually takes place in bringing about the various phenomena, good and bad, with which we are here dealing. Both emotion and behavior are produced by thought. This is generally known and accepted. But what is not so well known is that thought is actually a process in which an individual speaks to himself. Jacobson demonstrated this very clearly in his relaxation procedures. When the organs connected with speech are relaxed, thinking ceases.

Now, we have already put this knowledge to use in our procedures for taking the initial step in learning to cope with emotional and behavior problems and their effects. Up to this time most sufferers have been saying to themselves that their real suffering is the result of their emotional and behavior problems and their physical effects. We have sought to take the first step in stopping this suffering, aside from a purely religious approach, by telling the sufferer to say to himself that the failure to properly use his conditionability is his real problem. In the next step, we consolidate the progress that has been made, however small, by chopping destructive thoughts to pieces and uprooting them. That is, we tell ourselves that what we have been saying to ourselves in the past is not true.

Challenge the Old Self-Talk!

Again, using what is natural as our guide, it is certainly not natural to think that you can successfully speak new words to yourself without first rooting out the old words, which, because they are prior and were spoken to the self at the most impressionable age of childhood and repeated over many years, became firmly entrenched in your memory and consciousness. The failure to root out negative thoughts and inadequate self-images accounts for the relative ineffectiveness of some of the most popular therapies advocated in our generation.

After taking the previous step of enabling yourself to switch your attention on to the real problem, continue taking the initiative by uprooting and destroying as much as possible all the old self-talk which seeks to maintain your problems and to keep your attention focused on them. You do this by singling out all the old destructive sentences that you are continually repeating to yourself, and exposing them in the light of truth and reality for what they really are: absolutely false sentences which acquired their distortions through the improper use of the kind of conditionability with which you were born.

When you find yourself under stress which is producing your emotional and behavior problems, immediately seek to find out what the improper use of your conditionability has been forcing you to say to yourself. Because easily-conditioned and difficult-to-condition individuals are saying different sentences to themselves, we need to set up different programs for each, even though there are large areas of similarity due to the grandiose feelings that both have acquired.

Accordingly, if you are a basically easily-conditioned individual and are experiencing emotional problems or even feel one coming on, then try immediately to listen in to yourself to determine what you are saying to yourself. This may be a little difficult at first for you to do, but it will give you a head start if you look for sentences which you know to be a probable exaggeration. In other words, look for sentences which are telling you the worst things that could happen to you. A few examples will help. Look for sentences like the following:

"Something terrible is happening to me!"

"I can't stand it!"

"I will make a fool out of myself before all these people!"

"What will people think?"

"I should not have done it."

"How horrible of me to have done such a thing!"

"I don't deserve to be treated this way!"

"I can't understand why people don't recognize my good points!"

"This should not be so difficult for me!"

51

"Why should this bad thing have happened to me?"

"I can't help it, 'cause that's the way I am!"

When you discover sentences like that floating around in your mind, then immediately counteract each sentence with one that is less extreme, is not exaggerated, and states the truth about the matter. For example, counter the sentences just given with the following:

"Nothing terrible is happening to me. I am exaggerating the matter only because I have been using my conditionability incorrectly."

"I can stand it. I think I can't only because I have been using my conditionability incorrectly."

"I won't make a fool of myself. I think I will only because I have been using my conditionability incorrectly."

"I should not be so concerned about what people think of me. I think I

should only because I have been using my conditionability incorrectly."

"I should not expect perfection of myself. I think I should only because I have been using my conditionability incorrectly."

"What I have done is not horrible. I think it is only because I have been been using my conditionability incorrectly."

"It is not terrible that I am being mistreated. I think it is only because I have been using my conditionability incorrectly."

"I don't have to have people recognize my good points. I feel that I do only because I have been using my conditionability incorrectly."

"Things should not always be easy for me. I think they should only because I have been using my conditionability incorrectly."

"I don't need the attention of others. I think I do only because I have

been using my conditionability incorrectly."

"I should not expect that only good must happen to me. I feel that I should only because I have been using my conditionability incorrectly."

"I should take some responsibility for being what I am. I think I shouldn't only because I have been using my conditionability incorrectly."

If you are a basically difficult-to-condition individual and you experience a behavior problem or are tempted to behave in an unacceptable manner, then try immediately to listen in to yourself to determine what you are saying to yourself. This may be a little difficult at first, but you will get the idea if you look for sentences which you know to be a minimizing of the importance which others place upon the situation. Look for sentences which are telling you not to think so seriously about your behavior. Look for sentences something like the following:

"Why shouldn't I do what I want to do?"

"I have to do this to be happy!"

"It's everyone for himself in this world!"

"He (or she) isn't any better than I am!"

"Doing it just this once won't hurt!"

"I'll try it just to see what happens!"

"It's all their fault!"

"It's too hard to act any other way!"

"This world owes me a living!"

"I was born to be on top!"

"My decisions are always right!"

When you discover sentences like the above gaining your attention, as you surely will, then immediately counteract each sentence with one that is more serious and more responsible as we do in the following:

"I can't always do what I want to. I feel that I can only because I have been using my conditionability incorrectly."

"I don't have to do what I want to do to be happy. I feel that I must only

because I have been using my conditionability incorrectly."

"I must not be concerned only about myself. I feel that I must only because I have been using my conditionability incorrectly."

"It is not true that no one is better than I am. I think that is true only because I have been using my conditionability incorrectly."

"I must observe the rules. When I think I do not have to, it is only because I have been using my conditionability incorrectly."

"I should not take any unnecessary risks. I think I can only because I have been using my conditionability incorrectly."

"I must not blame others for my wrong behavior. When I do, it is only because I have been using my conditionability incorrectly."

"It is not too difficult to act the right way. I think it is only because I *have been using my conditionability incorrectly."*

"The world does not owe me a living. I think it does only because I have been using my conditionability incorrectly."

"I was not born to be on top. I feel that I was only because I have been using my conditionability incorrectly."

"My decisions are not always right. I think they always are only because I have been using my conditionability incorrectly."

Of course, easily-conditioned individuals also have occasional behavior problems, but they need to respond to them as they do to their emotional problems; there is little possibility that they will not take them seriously enough. And difficult-to-condition individuals also have occasional emotional problems, but they need to respond to them as they do to their behavior problems; there is little probability that they will take them too seriously.

But the important thing is to immediately, on the spot, counteract the untrue sentences as soon as you ferret them out. If you do this consistently, they will lose their power to enlarge your emotional and behavior problems or to maintain them at their present troublesome level. The old self-talk is rooted out.

But we want to be able to do even more to the old self-talk. We want to minimize the possibility of its arising in the first place. Toward that end, the next suggestion is given.

Implant the New Self-Talk!

Just as it is part of the nature of the way human behavior operates that problems occur when we say incorrect sentences to ourselves, even so it is the natural way to replace the old wrong sentences with new correct ones if we are to solve our problems. This is what we attempt in this next suggestion.

It is difficult to separate what is suggested in the previous section from what is suggested in this one. Perhaps we can do so if we remember that the challenge to the old self-talk is to be used primarily as an on-the-spot countering action in times of stress, while the implanting of the new self-talk, as suggested here, is designed especially to be used on a regular-schedule basis, preferably when not under stress. While the previous suggestion was aimed primarily at amelioration, the present one is aimed primarily at prevention. The previous suggestion was largely a defensive tactic, dealing with negatives, while the present suggestion largely takes the offensive and deals with positives.

The suggestion here revolves about the implanting of positive sentences, using techniques that have been utilized by a number of therapists. The sentences themselves are based on Natural Therapy's view of the origin and solution of emotional and behavior problems. The technique for implanting them is primarily an adaptation of a technique used in a program called Thought Dynamics, headed by California psychologist William Tanner and his associates.

In preparation for using these psychological techniques, we must first fashion the kinds of sentences which will represent the new self-talk, or the new statements which we need to repeat to ourselves. Again it is necessary to fashion sentences of two kinds: some for easily-conditioned individuals and some for difficult-to-condition individuals.

I suggest the following for use by easily-conditioned individuals. You will note that they seek to assist the individual to use his conditionability to help others. How they are to be used will be explained a little later. Here are sample sentences:

> *"I can change my feelings by changing the sentences I repeat to myself!"*

> *"I get my own needs satisfied to the extent I help others meet theirs!"*

> *"I enjoy emotional peace as I use my conditionability, as nature intended, primarily to serve the interests of others!"*

> *"I enjoy emotional peace as I use my seriousness, as nature intended, primarily to adequately assess the needs of others and help them as much as I can!"*

> *"I enjoy emotional peace as I use my tendency for introspection, as nature intended, primarily to determine if I am doing what I can to help others!"*

"I enjoy emotional peace as I use my tender-mindedness, as nature intended, primarily to have sympathy for the needs of others and to help them fulfill them!"

"I enjoy emotional peace as I use my carefulness, as nature intended, primarily to be as thorough as possible in helping others!"

"I enjoy emotional peace as I use my reliability, as nature intended, primarily to carry out my intentions to help others!"

"I enjoy emotional peace as I use my tendency to be pessimistic, as nature intended, primarily to do all I can to make certain that others are properly helped and leave nothing to chance!"

"I enjoy emotional peace as I use all of my characteristics, as nature intended, primarily to further the interests of humankind!"

Many, if not all, of the sentences above may apply to your situation. You can probably think of others that need to be added in your case. Extend the list by composing some of your own, always aiming your characteristics primarily toward a concern for others. Try to express them in the present tense and as positively as possible.

Before continuing with directions for their use, let me list some sample sentences that apply especially to difficult-to-condition individuals.

> *"I can change my behavior by changing some of the sentences I have been repeating to myself!"*

> *"I get my own needs satisfied better as I help others meet theirs!"*

> *"I am able to behave correctly as I use my conditionability, as nature intended, primarily for the benefit of others!"*

> *"I am able to behave correctly as I use my carefree attitude, as nature intended, primarily to do daring things that are necessary to better our world!"*

> *"I am able to behave correctly as I use my tough-mindedness, as nature*

intended, primarily to do difficult things that must be done to help others!"

"I am able to behave correctly as I use my natural aggressiveness, as nature intended, primarily to get those things started that are necessary to be done to help humankind!"

"I am able to behave correctly as I use my daring, as nature intended, primarily to challenge the rules, if necessary, to help a person in need!"

"I am able to behave correctly as I use my tendency to act without deliberation, as nature intended, primarily to go into action to help those in need of immediate help, while others are still thinking it over!"

"I am able to behave correctly as I use my over-optimism, as nature intended, primarily to give at least a try to certain things that might help people!"

"I am able to behave correctly as I use my need to be the center of attraction,

*as nature intended, primarily to
call attention to an urgent need in
our world!"*

Again, be sure to add sentences that meet
special behavior needs that you have and
which express the urgency of using the qualities you have primarily in the interest of
others. Make certain that they are expressed
positively and in the present tense.

Now assemble the sentences you feel you
need (there may be as few as five or as many
as thirty), and write or type each sentence
on a separate small card, or record them on
a tape cassette at least twenty seconds apart.
Now use them in the three ways we suggest
below.

1. Speak and visualize your new
sentences to yourself.

Once you have your sentences available
as suggested, then read (aloud, if possible)
each sentence, or listen to it on your cassette
player. Then visualize yourself feeling or
acting as the sentence suggests, visualizing
as vividly and in as great detail as possible
for twenty seconds. (You can realize the

64

importance of visualizing when you remember what Jacobson found about thinking — that thinking is a form of speaking to yourself in which, besides the tongue, the eyes are importantly involved.)

Repeat the reading (listening) and visualizing procedure for each sentence on your list until all of them have been read (listened to) and visualized. And repeat the entire procedure at least three times a day, preferably in the morning, at midday, and at night. You are encouraged, however, to do it as often as possible each day because the more often you do it the greater the results you will achieve. Don't do it in a rote manner but with meaning and deliberation.

2. Relax and implant your most important sentences under the most receptive conditions.

There is good evidence that, when we are relaxed, we are more mentally and emotionally receptive, so at least once a day, perhaps right before you fall asleep at night, relax your mind and body as deeply as possible. A good book on relaxation (such as the Jacobson books listed in the references) can teach you how to do this. When you are as relaxed as you can possibly succeed in being, then drop one or more of your most important sentences into your relaxed consciousness, preferably by repeating them aloud and with deliberation several times. As you do this, take time after each sentence to visualize yourself fulfilling the sentence clearly, in great detail, and as realistically as possible. The more often you are able to do this each day, the more effective it is.

3. Act out your sentences.

This third procedure is the most important one, for it is the final goal of all the preceding steps. Begin by acting out your most important sentence, at first for one-half hour each day. As time passes, the half-hour of acting out the sentence will tend to lengthen naturally, till it almost by itself tends to act itself out whenever there is an opportunity for it to do so during the remainder of the day. Once it reaches that point (don't be impatient), add the next most important sentence and follow the same procedure. Do this until all your sentences tend to act themselves out as the opportunities for them to do so present themselves.

If you are fortunate to be in a job or a location where there is abundant opportunity to help others, this last procedure will be easy. If you can change to a job or location where there is a greater opportunity to do so, you are also fortunate. If opportunities at your job are limited, you can make helping others your avocation, using your free time to help others. Actually, there is hardly anyone who cannot do something to help others.

It is easy to start practicing your new behavior on members of your family. It is a mistake, however, to stop there, for in one sense the members of your family are an extension of yourself, and it really becomes a matter of furthering only your own interests in a way. So be sure to extend your concern and help as widely as possible. There is practically no likelihood that you will overdo it, as long as you understand that your particular kind of conditionability, while it is to be used primarily for the welfare of others, is also to be used for your own welfare. Anyway, there is likely to be enough grandiosity remaining to prevent you from neglecting your own welfare as you go about furthering the welfare of others.

Natural Therapy is Summarized

It is evident to you by this time that Natural Therapy, as described in this chapter, works because it is in harmony with nature. It is natural law that, when conditionability is used solely or primarily for one's own interests, it produces an unnatural grandiosity that brings on emotional and behavior problems. Problems of that kind are prevented or eliminated when natural conditionability is used, as nature intended, primarily for the survival and betterment of all mankind.

That nature works that way is largely confirmed also by no less a person than Dr. Hans Selye, the world's foremost authority on stress, who holds that it is scientifically true that if we practice what he calls altruistic egotism — showing interest in our fellow humans because it is in our interest to do so — we will be free from destructive stress (see his book listed in the references). It is based on natural law, Dr. Selye claims, and, like natural law which keeps the planets in orbit, it works to keep people on their proper course.

But there is one aspect of nature that can provide an added dimension to Natural Therapy. It stems from the natural knowledge of God that so many, if not all, people possess. Adding God to Natural Therapy, as we do in the ensuing chapter, provides us with an opportunity to employ the total human — body, mind, and spirit — in the conquest of emotional and behavior problems.

Chapter Three

NATURAL THERAPY
AND
RELIGION

This is Some Preliminary Information

Hans Eysenck, whose experimental work underlies much of Natural Therapy, and Albert Ellis, whose clinical work partly confirms some of the ideas included in Natural Therapy, would disown many things in this chapter, for both regard religion as irrational. Camilla Anderson, whose ideas about grandiosity with some alterations are important in Natural Therapy, finds that some parts of the Judaeo-Christian religion in symbolic form are very useful in her therapy. The contention of this chapter is that religion, when correctly used, is very effective in the solution of emotional and behavior problems. When it is added to the Natural Therapy described in the previous chapter, Natural Therapy's effectiveness is improved considerably.

But easily-conditioned and difficult-to-condition individuals ordinarily are not able to effectively use the help that religion can offer. That is usually because of their grandiosity, which does not permit them to sufficiently use that part of religion which could have prevented their problems to begin with, and which now can supply the best means of alleviating them. In this chapter we point out how this seeming dilemma can be solved.

Since the term "religion" is an ambiguous one, meaning different things to different people, it is helpful to use one specific form of religion to illustrate the proper use of religion for emotional and behavior problems. And for that purpose I have chosen Biblical Christianity. Biblical Christianity is a good choice because it is the most common form (with variations) of religion in our country and one with which most Americans are familiar. It is also the religion with which I am most familiar, having been a pastor in one branch of it for over thirty years. And, most importantly, in my opinion it is the form of religion which can offer the most help for emotional and behavior problems.

Other forms of religion, of course, can help, but it is our experience that they help in the measure that they approach what Biblical Christianity can offer. Even though your cherished religion may not be Biblical Christianity, I am certain that, as we apply Biblical Christianity here, you will be able to note how you can more effectively use your own brand of religion for your problems.

Acquire a Religious Faith

It is likely that most of you, especially the easily-conditioned ones among you, already have a religious faith of some kind. If you don't have one, or if you are in some doubt as to whether you do (easily-conditioned and difficult-to-condition individuals sometimes have such doubts), the best advice I can give is that you contact a clergyman or a church to get help in acquiring a faith.

Biblical Christianity is most useful for easily-conditioned and difficult-to-condition individuals to acquire a religious faith. Easily-conditionable people often have neurotic guilt, and the Gospel of full and free forgiveness through faith in Christ, which is the heart of Biblical Christianity, offers the most satisfactory answer to the problem of guilt, and the easily-conditioned sufferer is likely to respond to it quite eagerly.

Difficult-to-condition people ordinarily do not have significant feelings of guilt, and they are inclined to shy away from religion, knowing its opposition to much of their type of behavior. In that case, Biblical Christianity advocates the use of God's Law to engender proper feelings of guilt in order to bring about a feeling of need for the Gospel. When the Gospel is accepted, no matter how weakly or strongly, the individual is in possession of forgiveness and has a saving faith.

Biblical Christianity offers one more help to the acquiring of faith. It assures the searcher for faith that God's Spirit is actively at work through the Law and the Gospel, seeking to bring about such a saving faith.

How Strong Does Faith Have To Be?

Those who suffer from emotional and behavior problems usually think that their religion is not helping them as it has promised

76

because their faith is not strong enough. I recall one very faithful church member who was suffering so much from emotional problems that she was plunged into despair, thinking that she no longer had faith.

Actually, it is not the strength of faith that is most important. Jesus said (Matthew 17:20) that if we have only a very small faith (the size of a grain of mustard seed), we will be able to remove mountains. The important thing is to apply faith. While a strong faith is better than a weak one, it won't do any good if it is not applied. If your faith does not seem to be working, it is probably due to the fact that you are not applying it to the place where it needs to be applied to bring results.

That is apparently the lesson that Jesus taught when, on several occasions, He referred to His disciples as people "of little faith." There is no doubt that their faith in Him as the Messiah was very strong, for they had forsaken all to follow Him. Yet when they were in temporal need and danger, somehow they did not apply their faith to those situations. If they had, it would have assured them that God had a plan for their life, that such things as storms and food and clothing were under His control, that whatever He decided about the situation would be best, etc. It is no wonder that Jesus called their faith "little." It is interesting to note that the word Jesus used, which is translated as "little," was a word that most often means "few." In that sense Jesus was referring to His disciples as believers "who applied their faith to only a few areas of their lives."

Be assured that if you have a religious faith, or had one, and it has not worked to solve your problems, it is not because your faith is, or was, not strong enough. And if you are one who is just thinking about or in the process of acquiring a religious faith, do not be deterred by any thought that you might not be able to acquire a strong enough faith. Rather, take heart at the knowledge that as long as you have a religious faith, you have something that is a starting point for the best solution to your problems: the desire, however weak, to do God's will.

You Must Do God's Will

Once you have a faith, no matter how weak, it is important to know and to do God's will.

Of course, the most important part of God's will for you is your own salvation. But once you have come to faith, you are in possession of salvation, and, from that point on, it is God's will that, out of love and gratitude to Him, you center your life about loving God above all and your neighbor as yourself, using the gifts, abilities, and characteristics that you have primarily for those purposes. To the extent that you do, you will escape significant emotional and behavior problems.

To understand this more fully, consider the following. It is easy to understand why those without a religious faith are more apt to have emotional and behavior problems. Without a religious faith, grandiosity is unopposed in its compulsions that force the individual to use his characteristics exclusively for self-aggrandizement. Because this leads the individual to act contrary to God's will, God seeks to correct the individual by permitting emotional and behavior problems to enter his life to signal to him that he is acting incorrectly and must change his behavior to conform to His will.

But He permits emotional and behavior problems to enter also into the life of those who have a religious faith, but usually only under the following circumstances. An easily-conditioned or difficult-to-condition person acquires a faith, perhaps especially because his grandiosity is interested in receiving from such faith the personal assurances that come from the promise of forgiveness, of God's providence, and of eternal life. In that way he is little different from anyone who becomes interested in religion. And he enjoys the blessings, like the above, that his faith offers.

But a certain amount of grandiosity usually remains, enough in some cases to prevent his love and gratitude to God for all the afore-mentioned blessings from inducing him to give adequately of himself in return. To be sure, there is always some response to the blessing of faith, and the easily-conditioned and the difficult-to-condition believer, like the moderately-conditionable believer, find it possible — yes, even rewarding — to carry out God's will in things that are not overly important or not too demanding.

But the Creator equipped the easily-conditioned and the difficult-to-condition people as He did primarily that they might use their special equipment to glorify Him by carrying out His will for the spiritual and temporal welfare of humankind. The still-partly-grandiose and easily-conditioned believer exaggerates the importance of it all to the point where he is scared out by his fear of failure. The still-partly-grandiose and difficult-to-condition believer does not recognize its importance and ignores it. Both are aware, however, that it makes some demands on them, and, because they feel that things should be easy for them, they lose interest.

So, even as in the case of the person without faith, God permits emotional and behavior problems to enter the life of those with faith when they don't apply it properly to the will of God for their life. When the easily-conditioned believer fails to do what he can do to carry out God's will, he is apt to feel neurotic guilt which produces emotional problems. When the difficult-to-condition believer fails to do what he can do to carry out God's will, apparently without punishment by God and even forgiven for his failures, he is likely to be even less responsible in his behavior, and behavior problems occur.

Thus there may be nothing wrong with the sufferer's religious faith; he is only failing to apply it to every area of his life. He is not trusting God's direction for his life — it does not appeal to whatever grandiosity he still has. So he fails to follow God's direction, and problems are inevitable. But he still has a faith, and that is still the starting point for the best way to eliminate emotional and behavior problems, as we shall see.

This Is How To Get Started

Now that I have demonstrated how emotional and behavior problems can arise in spite of a religious faith, and why it is difficult to eliminate emotional and behavior problems even when faith is present, I now proceed to show how a religious faith, properly applied, can actually provide the most effective solution to such problems. I have demonstrated in the foregoing how remaining grandiosity prevents the proper application of religious faith to the area where it needs to be applied. Now I show how such grandiosity can be induced to apply faith to the proper area. In doing so, I need to describe the important part that conditionability plays in religious faith.

We mentioned earlier that it was your grandiosity that prevented you from using your religion correctly to solve your problems. Your grandiosity responds to religion when it evidently offers something in return. It tends to reject religion when it appears to make demands that appear to oppose grandiosity, as when it demands that a believer do God's will instead of his own. But God also has a way of getting around such obstacles. God catches your grandiosity slightly off guard by assuring you that your troubles are an indication of His love. Like a parent who corrects his child, He does so because He loves you.

Oh, if you had a religious faith, you knew that already, but you just could not fully accept it. Because of your still-remaining grandiosity, you insisted that everything about your life should be just as you wanted it, without any troubles at all. But God has a way of changing all that. When God permits your problems to escalate to the point where you begin to feel that you cannot function as you feel you have to, after trying everything else to be rid of your problem and failing, you are willing to reconsider the role of His will for your life, even as you are doing right now.

And, lo and behold, when you do, something marvelous begins to happen. It starts to make sense that God has a plan for your life, and that everything works together for good to them that love God. You begin to realize what all of this means. He so fashioned you and your life that it gave you every opportunity to carry out your life's most important purpose: to glorify God by being His instrument in furthering His will for the temporal and eternal welfare of humankind. He did everything possible to induce you to fit into His plan. He bestowed great blessings when you did, and He tried to correct you when you didn't.

He even chose you to be a leader and to play a special role in carrying out His plan for the temporal and eternal welfare of mankind. He saw to it that you were born with the kind of conditionability that would enable you to develop qualities that are so important to the welfare of mankind. The Creator, whose government and providence rules the earth, as Biblical Christians believe, would not leave the part that humans were to play in His plans for the universe to the probability and chance that is inherent in behavior-conditioning by fallible human beings. He would make certain that His will for the survival and progress of humankind would be carried out by not entrusting the most important aspect of His plan principally to humans who could be conditioned to fail in this important task. By creating humans who, because it was in their genes and chromosomes, would be compelled to be concerned about human needs and also to act to restrain harmful excesses, and humans who, because it was their biological nature, would be compelled to take the necessary risks, the Ruler of the Universe, for the benefit of His creatures, insured that human survival would be assured and human progress would be made. And He chose you to have such qualities and to use them as best you can for that purpose.

Now your whole past life begins to make sense. Since your whole life is part of God's plan for you and humankind, even though He permitted you to become grandiose and work primarily for your own self-aggrandizement, it may be that, despite your intentions, God was using even this to work toward the benefit of others. Many a grandiose person, though working only in his own interest, can take consolation from the fact that God may have been using him to benefit others. Perhaps you have been so used.

But even if you can see no contribution for good in anything that your grandiosity has impelled you to do in the past, God is also using your failure as part of His plan to use you for good. Because of those past failures, He is motivating you to be more zealous than you could ever have been without them to now use your special qualities to carry out His will for the spiritual and temporal welfare of humankind.

That plan of God is still working in your life as you have been led by God to read this book, which is now helping you to understand and appreciate the great blessing that your conditionability really is.

"But," the Bible-oriented Christian may ask, "if conditionability is so important, why isn't it mentioned in the Bible, and why has God not enabled us to discover its importance sooner?" Consider the following.

Is Conditionability in the Bible?

In the first place, it really is not necessary that God should have made a special revelation of the existence or even the importance of degree of conditionability in the Bible or through the laboratories of Hans Eysenck. The important thing is to know that we can prevent or solve our emotional and behavior problems if we use our biological equipment for the purposes that God intended. And that knowledge God has made abundantly clear in the Bible. But, as long as some of you may be concerned about it, it is my conviction that the Bible regards variable conditionability and its importance as a very common, natural, and obvious aspect of human nature.

When I first was impressed by Eysenck's theory of extraversion-introversion, I began to search the Bible for references to it. In a recent letter from Eysenck, he also expressed interest in knowing what Scripture had to say about it. I found that, while the Bible does not make a special point to fully describe conditionability and the part it plays in human behavior and only refers to it in passing, there are, as you would expect, abundant examples of its existence and of its effects upon human behavior. For example, if Adam and Eve were the first parents of the human race, we would expect that in their genetic makeup could be found genes for extraversion, introversion, and ambiversion. We can't look into their genetic makeup, but we may be able to make some judgments about it from their actions. It seems likely that they were both ambiverts, as one might expect. Blaming the serpent and even God for their transgression is a typical extravert (difficult conditionability) maneuver. At the same time, when they clothed themselves with fig leaves in a vain effort to hide their felt guilt, they displayed a typical introvert (easy conditionability) behavior. Neither of these actions were extreme ones and were thus typical of ambiverts. Cain (the extravert whose sacrifice was not acceptable to God) slew (extravert act) his brother Abel (the introvert whose sacrifice was pleasing to the Lord). Typically extravert, Cain does not appear to have been troubled by guilt, but he feared that others might harm him. Esau (the extravert) sold his birthright for a mess of pottage (an extravert act) to Jacob (the introvert), who later worked an unbelievable number of years (introvert behavior) to acquire pious (introvert) Rachel as his bride. Examples like these, taken from the beginning of the Bible, are found throughout the Bible from beginning to end.

Looking at the behavior of individuals in the Bible from the viewpoint of conditionability makes it more understandable and believable. I never understood the anguish expressed in the penitential psalms until I realized that they were the expressions of high introverts (easily-conditioned people). I now also understand Scripture's description of a class of people in Acts 7:51: "Ye stiffnecked and uncircumcised in heart and ears, ye do always resist the Holy Ghost: as your fathers did, so do ye." These people evidently were high extraverts (difficult-to-condition people, as people who reject religion often are), who inherited their extraversion from their parents. I could go on citing many additional examples.

One Bible passage that over the years has made Bible-oriented Christians very zealous about the importance of conditioning in the Christian education and training of their children is Proverbs 22:6, which is translated in the King James Version as follows: "Train up a child in the way he should go: and when he is old, he will not depart from it." But, as Jay Adams claims, a more accurate translation of this passage is: "Train a child after the manner of his way." This makes all the difference in the world, for it really says that if you train a child in the way he naturally wants to behave, he will behave that way in later life. With this more accurate translation, you can readily note that this passage tends to confirm the primacy of basic conditionability of the individual in behavior formation. In fact, it also bears out what we have been claiming throughout this book, that behavior is 80 to 85 percent hereditary and only about 15 to 20 percent environmental.

Again, there is a hint of the primacy of basic conditionability in the passage in Romans 2:15 where St. Paul says that when the conscience of the Gentiles acts up, their thoughts will either accuse them or excuse them. You immediately recognize that the former reaction is typical of easily-conditioned individuals, while the latter reaction exemplifies the difficult-to-condition person. So there is, after all, considerable Biblical evidence for the concept of conditionability and its importance.

Why has God made us wait until now to discover the importance of conditionability? I do not know. You might also ask: Why did He wait so long to permit us to discover anesthesia, penicillin, electricity, nuclear fission? It seems to be His way to permit us to discover important things when we need them most or when we can make the best use of them. Be that as it may, it is time to apply what we have thus far explained about religion and conditionability.

This Is How Your Conditionability Affects Your Religious Outlook

Although the King James translation of II Timothy 2:15 is not completely accurate, St. Paul there urges the young preacher Timothy to "rightly divide the word of truth," and many have taken that to be an exhortation to correctly divide and properly apply God's Word by using the Law at the proper time and place and the Gospel at the proper time and place. Paul, especially in the book of

Romans, consistently shows the difference between the two and urges that each be applied properly. There is a difference between their application to people before they come to faith and after they come to faith. We have already described how they are used properly in bringing people to faith. Here we are interested in how they are to be applied *after* coming to faith.

We have already pointed out that the easily-conditioned and the difficult-to-condition believer, who has problems in the area of emotion and behavior, has these problems because of the grandiosity that remains even after he comes to faith. If the easily-conditioned believer could be satisfied with the Gospel, he would largely lose his grandiosity. But because he is easily conditioned and because negative things make a greater impression on him than positive things, he, although he accepts the Gospel and is thus in possession of a saving faith, cannot entirely forgive himself and still insists upon behaving perfectly to assure himself of his worthiness. In the process he becomes more concerned about the Law than the Gospel, and thus prevents the elimination of his grandiosity through the acceptance of himself as forgiven, as he really is.

If the difficult-to-condition believer could adequately feel the need, as a redeemed child of God, to live in accordance with God's will, he would also lose his grandiosity. But because he is difficult to condition and is rather unimpressed by any requirements that are imposed from without, he, although he accepts the Gospel quite readily and is thus in possession of a saving faith, ignores the importance of also doing God's will and thus prevents the elimination of his grandiosity. Thus, though he is a person with a saving faith, he concentrates on the Gospel at the expense of the Law, unlike his counterpart, the easily-conditioned believer, who concentrates on the Law at the expense of the Gospel.

To be sure, it no doubt does happen that God can and does perform miracles and grants to some who are easily-conditioned or difficult-to-condition an adequate religious outlook notwithstanding. Others do acquire an adequate religious outlook because they realize the part that their conditionability plays. But, by and large, many have lacked either a miracle or a proper insight or both.

In addition, God, for His own good purposes, may decide to allow an inadequate religious outlook. As indicated earlier, He may permit grandiosity to remain enough to compel a person to act in ways which will further God's good and gracious will for mankind. But He does not do so indiscriminately. He does so only where the believer is able to bear up under the strain of the problems that are inherent in such situations. It is possible that you are one whom He has been using in this way. The fact that you are reading this book is an indication that you have been able to bear the burden, just as He has said. But now, also, He is indicating to you that such a burden no longer needs to be borne, for an important part that He has chosen you to play is now completed to His satisfaction and, in the light of that knowledge, you can look forward to whatever He still has in store for you with greater anticipation than ever.

Now You Are Ready to Deal With Your Problems

You are now ready to put religion to work on your emotional and behavior problems.

Some of you may try to use it, as pastors and churches commonly do, by applying God's Law and Gospel properly, although you are now aware how difficult it is for you to do so because of your kind of conditionability. This time, however, knowing what obstacles you have been placing in the way of God's Spirit working effectively in you to lead you to do God's will, perhaps you will achieve better results and lose your grandiosity and the problems it is causing you.

If this does not help, you will just have to proceed on whatever love and gratitude to God you have, to try to do God's will for you and to try to promote the spiritual and temporal good of your fellow humans as best you can. If your problems are very recent and of rather short duration, you may be able to start to do this immediately without any further preparation, and obtain good results. There is an often-overlooked, but very important, Biblical principle involved here. In John 7:17, Jesus promises that if anyone desires to do God's will (implying that he will do it), he will become convinced of the truth of God's Word. So, if you do God's will out of a desire to do so that is born of your love and gratitude to Him for your faith, however small it may be at this time, you will become more convinced of the truth of what God has said. And this includes the truth that God has a plan for your life, and that part of it is that you carry out His will and that you be His instrument in furthering the spiritual and temporal welfare of humankind, using your special qualities primarily for that purpose.

But probably the largest majority of you have had problems of long standing. You have formed thinking, emoting, and acting habits that are deeply ingrained, and it is difficult for you to break those habits. Under such conditions, any attempts to think, emote, and act differently at once are likely to end in failure. But all this can still be changed; it takes a little more time, and it needs to be done through the formation of new habits of thinking, emoting, and acting. The use of religious truth for that purpose makes that task easier because it provides greater motivation, and God has promised to help. The suggestions in the next three sections, while they can be used for any kinds of emotional and behavior problems, are especially useful for the more difficult ones.

Switch the Focus to the Real Problem!

Up to now you have been preoccupied with your emotional and behavior problems and their physical effects. If you have been a religious person in the past, you may even have added an additional concern as a result of the fact that your religion did not seem to be helping you. You may have doubts about your faith.

Take the terror out of all this by following the suggestions made in the previous chapter under the section titled *Switch the Focus to the Real Problem!* on page 38. But remember that now, in addition to all that is stated there, you also have the assurance that God Himself will be at work in the program outlined in the remainder of this chapter.

Challenge the Old-Self Talk!

You see, behind your emotions and behavior are your thoughts, and they are nothing but self-talk. If you have not done so, get started on this suggestion by reading what is said about it in the previous chapter under the section headed *Challenge the Old-Self Talk!* on page 49.

But now you are going one step further. You are going to challenge the old-self talk more strongly in the following manner. If you are an easily-conditioned person, oppose with a religious truth every exaggerated statement that you catch yourself making to yourself. Here are some examples:

"Nothing that happens to me, as a child of God, is ever awful, terrible, or catastrophic. I feel that is only because I have not been using my conditionability primarily for the purpose that God intended!"

"I can stand and take what is happening to me, since I am a child of God. I think I can't only because I have not been using my conditionability primarily for the purpose that God intended!"

"It really doesn't matter what people think of me. I feel that it does only because I have not been using my conditionability primarily for the purpose that God intended!"

"It really doesn't matter to me whether

people think of me at all. I think it does only because I have not been using my conditionability primarily for the purpose that God intended!"

"It doesn't really matter that I acted differently than I should have or could have. I feel that it does only because I have not been using my condition-ability primarily for the purpose that God intended!"

"What I have done is not horrible. I feel it is only because I have not been using my conditionability primarily for the purpose that God intended!"

"Why shouldn't I expect people to treat me harshly at times and overlook me? I feel that such things should never hap-pen to me only because I have not been using my conditionability primarily for the purpose that God intended!"

"Why should I be so upset when people don't recognize my good points? I get upset only because I have not been using my conditionability primarily for the purpose that God intended!"

"Why should things be easy for me? I think they should only because I have not been using my conditionability primarily for the purpose that God intended!"

"If it seems like I'm alone in this world, it is only because I have not been using my conditionability primarily for the purpose that God intended!"

"I should not expect that some misfortune should not befall me. I feel that I should experience no misfortune only because I have not been using my conditionability primarily for the purpose that God intended!"

"Things really are not as bad as I think they are. I have been led to think they are only because I have not been using my conditionability primarily for the purpose that God intended!"

If you are basically difficult-to-condition and experience a behavior problem or are tempted to behave improperly, then try immediately to listen in to determine what you are

100

saying to yourself. Then oppose each sentence with a religious truth somewhat as follows:

"I should not feel that I can always do what I want to do. I feel that I can only because I have not been using my conditionability primarily for the purpose that God intended!"

"I should not feel that I have to do this or that to be happy. I feel that I have to only because I have not been using my conditionability primarily for the purpose that God intended!"

"I should not feel that I should be concerned only about myself. I feel that way only because I have not been using my conditionability primarily for the purpose that God intended!"

"I should not feel that no one is better than I am. I feel that way only because I have not been using my condition-ability primarily for the purpose that God intended!"

"I should not feel that I need not always observe the rules. I feel that way only because I have not been using

my conditionability primarily for the purpose that God intended!"

"I should not take unnecessary risks. I do so only because I have not been using my conditionability primarily for the purpose that God intended!"

"I should not blame others for my behavior. I do this only because I have not been using my conditionability primarily for the purpose that God intended!"

"I should not feel that it is too difficult to act the right way. I feel that it is only because I have not been using my conditionability primarily for the purpose that God intended!"

"I should not feel that the world owes me a living. I feel that it does only because I have not been using my conditionability primarily for the purpose that God intended!"

"I should not feel that I was born to be on top. I feel that way only because I have not been using my condition-

ability primarily for the purpose that God intended!"

"I should not feel that my decisions are always right. I feel that they are only because I have not been using my conditionability primarily for the purpose that God intended!"

Again, because both easily-conditioned and difficult-to-condition believers also occasionally speak sentences to themselves that are more typical of their opposites, when that occurs the problems involved are not usually severe enough that they need any special attention. The important thing is to catch yourself saying the wrong things to yourself, and immediately oppose any distortion of the truth with a religious truth to the contrary. Of course, it is better if you can prevent such wrong self-talk from taking place at all. In what follows we seek to use religion to help bring that about.

Implant the New-Self Talk!

The procedure here is similar to the one I used rather successfully with a church group in a year-long experiment. The mechanics for its implementation are given in the previous chapter under the section titled *Implant the New-Self Talk!* which begins on page 58. However, one important feature is added to that: a religious truth is appended. So substitute the following sentences for the sentences given in the previous chapter.

If you are an easily-conditioned believer, substitute sentences like the following for each of the three activities (speak and visualize, relax and implant, and act out) suggested for this section.

> *"I can change my behavior by changing some of the sentences I have been repeating to myself, and God is helping me to do so!"*

> *"I get my needs satisfied better as I help others to meet theirs, and God is helping me to do so!"*

> *"I enjoy emotional peace as I use my conditionability, as God has intended, primarily to serve the interests of others!"*

> *"I enjoy emotional peace as I use my seriousness, as God intended,*

primarily to adequately assess the needs of others and to help them as much as I can!'"

"I enjoy emotional peace as I use my tendency for introspection, as God intended, primarily to determine if I am doing what I can to help others!'"

"I enjoy emotional peace as I use my tender-mindedness, as God intended, primarily to have sympathy for the needs of others and to help them fulfill those needs!'"

"I enjoy emotional peace as I use my carefulness, as God intended, primarily to be as thoughtful as possible in helping others!'"

"I enjoy emotional peace as I use my reliability, as God intended, primarily to carry out my intentions to help others!'"

"I enjoy emotional peace as I use my tendency to worry, as God intended, primarily to be concerned about the welfare of others!'"

"I enjoy emotional peace as I use my

tendency to fear, as God intended, primarily to become alert to the dangers that others face!"

"I enjoy emotional peace as I use my tendency to be pessimistic, as God intended, primarily to do all I can to make certain that others are properly helped, leaving nothing to chance!"

"I enjoy emotional peace as I use any of my special characteristics, as God intended, primarily in the interest of others!"

If you are a difficult-to-condition believer, substitute sentences like the following for use in each of the three activities (speak and visualize, relax and implant, and act out) suggested for use in this section:

"I can change my behavior by changing the sentences I have been repeating to myself, and God is helping me to do so!"

"I get my own needs satisfied as I help others to meet theirs, and God is helping me to do so!"

"I am able to behave correctly as I use

my conditionability, as God intended, primarily for the benefit of others!"

"I am able to behave correctly as I use my carefree attitude, as God intended, primarily to do daring things that are necessary to better our world!"

"I am able to behave correctly as I use my tough-mindedness, as God intended, primarily to cast aside obstacles that stand in the way of helping others!"

"I am able to behave correctly as I use my natural aggressiveness, as God intended, primarily to help get started the things that need to be done to help others!"

"I am able to behave correctly as I use my daring, as God intended, primarily to challenge the rules, if necessary, to help a person in real need!"

"I am able to behave correctly as I use my tendency to act without deliberation, as God intended, primarily to go into action to help those who need immediate help, while others

are still thinking it over!"

"I am able to behave correctly as I use my over-optimism, as God intended, primarily to at least give a try to some things about which there may be some doubt as to their ability to help others!"

"I am able to behave correctly as I use my need to be the center of attraction, as God intended, primarily to call attention to an urgent need in our world!"

"I am able to behave correctly as I use any of my special characteristics, as God intended, primarily for the benefit of humankind!"

Of course, always remember to make up additional sentences that meet more fully your own special needs and problems, making certain that they are in line with religious truth and are expressed positively and in the present tense. Always be sure to follow the three-fold and precise directions for their use: speak and visualize them, relax and implant them, and act them out.

108

Natural Therapy With Religion
is Summarized

The therapy suggested in this chapter is partly based on the Golden Rule which is advocated strongly by all the major religions of the world. Jesus teaches the Golden Rule in these words: "Whatsoever ye would that men should do to you, do ye even so to them" (Matthew 7:12). Taoism states: "Regard your neighbor's gain as your gain and regard your neighbor's loss as your own." The Jewish Talmud says: "What is hurtful to yourself, do not to your fellowman. This is the whole of the Torah. The remainder is but commentary." Islam states: "No one of you is a believer until he loves for his brother what he loves for himself." Confucianism holds: "Is there any one maxim which ought to be acted upon throughout one's whole life? Surely the maxim of lovingkindness is such. Do not unto others what you would not that they should do unto you." And Buddhism sums it all up as follows: "Hurt not others with that which pains yourself." While Natural Therapy goes beyond the Golden Rule by holding that easily-conditioned and difficult-to-condition believers are to use their special characteristics especially in the interest of others, the widespread advocating of the Golden Rule adds considerable weight to the Natural Therapy we have advocated in this chapter.

In addition, by using Biblical Christianity as our model, we have been able to add special incentives to use conditionability properly, incentives which are absent in the therapy suggested in the previous chapter — the additional motivation resulting from the knowledge that one's conditionability is the plan of an all-wise and loving Creator, that believers feel grateful enough to God for His love and forgiveness to have at least a small desire to do His will, that carrying out His will benefits our fellow humans not only temporally, but especially spiritually and eternally. Greater incentives than these would be difficult to find.

There is, therefore, no doubt that religion is not only a very natural part of therapy, but that it adds greatly to the effectiveness of therapy. Adding the wisdom, power, love, and will of God to the key factor of conditionability certainly provides the ultimate inducement to use conditionability more fully in the service of others, modifying grandiosity more effectively, providing a greater measure of true self-esteem for the easily-conditioned, and earning greater response and cooperation from others in helping the difficult-to-condition to properly meet their needs.

Does Natural Therapy Work?

We have already learned from the famed Dr. Hans Selye that altruistic egotism, which is largely the basis of Natural Therapy when used without religion, is scientifically demonstrated as a preventive for distress. We really did not need that scientific testimony, however, for history is replete with examples of men and women who have enjoyed some freedom from distress and have had a measure of inner peace as they dedicated their lives to the service of others. Life has always proved that it is better to give than to receive.

The Christian religion, whose principal teachings we have used to add spiritual factors to Natural Therapy, would never have survived and grown over the centuries as it has, if it did not produce even more favorable results. And its history, too, is replete with

111

accounts of men and women who have lived victorious lives by conforming to the will of God for them. They are demonstrations, everywhere visible, of the truth of Jesus' words: "He that saveth his life shall lose it, but he that loseth his life for My sake shall find it."

The therapy I suggest in this book is the culmination of my thirty-year search for a satisfactory solution to emotional and behavior problems. It is ironic that the answer lay in something that I had known about all my life but considered too simple to do so much.

AFTERWORD

AFTERWORD

Now that you have been rather thoroughly exposed to Natural Therapy, there is only one more thing to do, and that is to put its principles into practice in your life. I would be less than naive if I thought, as many therapists do, that since you now have, for the first time perhaps, been confronted with the kinds of information you need to have your problems solved, you would be more than anxious to get started on following the directions given in this book and to implement them faithfully. I've been through that experience so often that I know the obstacles that lie in your path.

As far as I know, no one has researched this strange phenomenon of a person who has been afflicted for a long time with emotional and behavior problems, confronted for the first time with a therapy that gives every indication of providing some real help, seemingly unable to find the energies to do what he must do to overcome his problems. A long time ago Alfred Adler observed this phenomenon among people with emotional problems; they generally appeared to him to be indolent. He made no attempt, as I remember, to explain which came first, the indolence or the emotional problem. Others have sought to explain the inability or reluctance to really attack personal problems by attributing it to fear of change; some people have lived so long with their problems that they actually fear to change. Still others have suggested that victims are reluctant to give up their symptoms because they provide socially acceptable excuses for evading more responsible behavior. Again, others see in this reluctance an unwillingness to give up suffering, using it as a means of self-punishment to atone for unresolved guilt. All of the above appear to be possible characteristics, especially of easily-conditioned people.

But what about difficult-to-condition people? I suppose the best explanation for their reluctance to seek to change their inappropriate behavior is their inability to admit that their behavior is really inappropriate behavior. To them, their behavior is not really that inappropriate. After all, they apparently enjoy all the attention it brings them. It is all part of that exciting life that they lead, and they need that excitement, even though the impartial observer can note only the harm it is doing.

All that has been stated above makes it quite clear that the unwillingness, reluctance, and apparent inability to initiate and to follow through a program designed to overcome emotional and behavior problems is really the result of grandiosity on the part of both the easily-conditioned and the difficult-to-condition. The highly-conditionable and therefore highly-suggestible person is getting his feelings of superiority and entitlement filled by maintaining the *status quo* and thereby garnering for himself security from the threat of change, sympathy for his helpless condition, an excuse for not taking responsibility and some relief from guilt through self-punishment. The difficult-to-condition person is getting his feelings of superiority and entitlement filled by all the attention he attracts to himself by his outlandish behavior, satisfying some of his compelling needs in the process. You've got to offer such people a great deal to induce them to give up their grandiosity. Besides, it takes effort, and grandiose people expect that everything should be easy for them.

In order for such sufferers to really overcome their problems, they simply must go into action, and there is only one sure way of overcoming the unwillingness, the reluctance, the apparent inability to go into meaningful action. It is to deliberately muster up enough courage to do what I now suggest. They must expose themselves honestly and fully to reality — fully confront themselves with the real facts of their situation. So, you easily-conditioned one, get started by telling yourself that you are full of fears and have worried unnecessarily; you have become panicky when it wasn't really necessary; you have felt inferior when you really did not have to; you have allowed yourself to be overconcerned needlessly about your health or whatever concerned you most. Confront yourself with the reality that you looked at things like that in an unrealistic way, and that therefore you need not fear to change them, you need not punish yourself for them, you need not use them as an excuse for your failures. Face up to these realities, and do so right now!

And, you difficult-to-condition person, get started by telling yourself that you create a lot of unnecessary trouble for yourself by always wanting your own way, by placing your own interests always before the interests of others, by failing to show the proper love and concern for your fellow humans. It is downright sinful that you give full rein to your own desires while you overlook the needs of others. And it doesn't have to be that way. You only act in that self-defeating manner because you have a wrong view of the way things really are. They are really more important and more serious than you think they are. Face up to that, and do so right now!

You see, you have to take yourself by the scruff of the neck and make yourself face the reality of the way things really are. Up to now, you have given yourself the benefit of any doubt about it. Now get tough with yourself. Get up enough nerve to have some level-headed person help you to face the way things really are. This kind of shock treatment is guaranteed to break grandiosity's control over you — at least to the extent that it will make you more willing and perhaps even eager to carry out all the directions given in the preceding chapters.

And finally, know that when you do, you will get some favorable results — some of you immediately, others of you more gradually. Don't be impatient. Results are guaranteed — not only by science, but by God Himself!

REFERENCES

Anderson, Camilla M. "The Pot and the Kettle," in O. Hobart Mowrer's *Morality and Mental Health*. Chicago: Rand McNally, 1967, pp. 196-202.

Anderson, Camilla M. "Guilt is Not the Problem," in *The Pastoral Counselor*, Fall, 1964.

Anderson, Camilla M. "The Self-Image: A Theory of the Dynamics of Behavior, Updated," in *Mental Hygiene*, 55 (July, 1971), pp. 365-68.

Ansbacher, Heinz L., and Rowena R. Ansbacher. *The Individual Psychology of Alfred Adler*. New York: Harper & Row, 1956.

Ansbacher, Heinz L., and Rowena R. Ansbacher, *Superiority and Social Interest*, Evanston: Northwestern University Press, 1970.

Ellis, Albert, and Robert A. Harper. *A New Guide to Rational Living*. Englewood Cliffs, N.J.: Prentice-Hall, Inc., 1975.

Eysenck, Hans J. *The Biological Basis of Personality*. Springfield, Ill.: Charles C. Thomas, 1967.

Eysenck, Hans J. *Crime and Personality*. Boston: Houghton Mifflin Co., 1964.

Eysenck, Hans J. *Fact and Fiction in Psychology*. Baltimore: Penguin Books, 1965.

Eysenck, Hans J. *Psychology Is About People*. London: The Penguin Press, 1972.

Eysenck, Hans J. *Readings in Extraversion-Introversion*, Vol. I. New York: John Wiley & Sons, Inc., 1970.

Eysenck, Hans J. *Readings in Extraversion-Introversion*, Vol. II. New York: John Wiley & Sons, Inc., 1971.

Eysenck, Hans J. *Readings in Extraversion-Introversion*, Vol. III. New York: John Wiley & Sons, Inc., 1971.

Eysenck, Hans J., and S. Rachman, *The Causes and Cures of Neurosis*. San Diego: R. R. Knapp, 1965.

Jacobson, Edmund. *Tension Control for Business Men*. New York: McGraw-Hill, 1963. (Paperback: Whitehall Co., Northbrook, Ill.)

Jacobson, Edmund. *You Must Relax*. New York: McGraw-Hill, 1957.

Selye, Hans. *Stress Without Distress*. Philadelphia: J. B. Lippincott Co., 1974.

Weekes, Claire. *Hope and Help for Your Nerves*. New York: Hawthorn Books, Inc., 1968.

Weekes, Claire. *Peace from Nervous Suffering*. New York: Hawthorn Books, Inc., 1972.